Contents

In Africa, promise and opportunity sit side by side with disease, war, and desperate poverty. This threatens both a core value of the United States—preserving human dignity—and our strategic priority—combating terror. American interests and American principles, therefore, lead in the same direction: we will work with others for an African continent that lives in liberty, peace, and growing prosperity. (President George W. Bush, 2002 National Security Strategy) [1]

INTRODUCTION

The terror attacks of 9/11 launched the United States into a deadly and costly war on terror against the al-Qaeda terrorist network. Prior to that fateful day, the United States had full knowledge of the organization, its aims, and its increasing levels of lethality. With thousands of casualties and billions of dollars spent on war in Afghanistan and Iraq, the question arises as to whether a long-term pre-emptive engagement to destroy the societal roots that allowed al-Qaeda to thrive would have been a more prudent investment.

The African continent is a hotbed for terrorist organizations. The prevalence of corruption, weak governance and poverty throughout Africa are prime targets for terrorist exploitation. [2] Additionally, religious and ethnic rivalries engender violence and create opportunities for extremist groups to form alliances with the local population. The Boko Haram is one such organization that seizes upon all of the aforementioned conditions to potentially destabilize the continent's most populous nation, Nigeria.

Currently, the U.S. State Department mission to Nigeria provides aid for a myriad of Nigeria's issues. However, a much more pervasive approach is necessary. U.S. Africa Command (AFRICOM) is the only organization with a leadership structure that incorporates both U.S. military and non-military sources of power solely for Africa. AFRICOM has the capability to structure efforts within Nigeria to anticipate, detect and prevent catastrophic attacks by Boko Haram. Such a victory would signify attainment of AFRICOM's Theater Strategic Objectives: defeat the Al-Qaeda terrorist organization and its associated networks;

1

ensure peace operation capacity exists to respond to emerging crises; cooperate with identified African states in the creation of an environment inhospitable to the unsanctioned possession and proliferation of WMD capabilities and expertise; improve security sector governance and increased stability through military support to comprehensive, holistic, and U.S. government efforts in designated states; and protect populations from deadly contagions.[3] To achieve these stated Theater Strategic Objectives, AFRICOM should implement Engagement Teams (ETs) to neutralize the foundation of the Boko Haram in Nigeria.

BACKGROUND

Boko Haram loosely translates to "Western Education is Sin" from West Africa's Hausa language. This Islamic militant group formed in 2002 in the capital of Nigeria's Borno state, Maiduguri. While known to the world as Boko Haram, the official name is "Jama'atu Ahlis Sunna Lidda'awati wal-Jihad" which translates from Arabic to "Group Committed to Propagating the Prophet's Teachings and Jihad."[4] Nigeria is officially a secular country. However, Borno state and the majority of northern states are predominantly Muslim, whereas the southern states are predominantly Christian.[5] In 2009, Boko Haram began resorting to violence to achieve its desired end state of creating an Islamic state based on Sharia law.

The world, including the Nigerian government, initially dismissed the Boko Haram as an insignificant organization due to its seemingly limited local area of operations in Northern Nigeria.[6] Following clashes with police in 2009 and the suspicious death of their founder, Mohammed Yusuf, while in police custody, Boko Haram attacks escalated from simple strikes with minimal casualties to mass killings.[7] In 2011, Boko Haram awakened the international community by bombing the United Nations (UN) building in Abuja, which killed 23 UN employees in August. Subsequently, a series of Christmas Day church bombings brought the death toll to 510 for 2011. U. S. Representative Patrick Meehan (R-Pa), as chair of the sub-committee on counter terrorism and intelligence, warned Congress not to underestimate the Boko Haram's capabilities to attack on U.S. soil; he specifically cited Congress' underestimation of Al Qaeda in the Arabian Peninsula (AQAP) and Tehrik-i-Taliban in Pakistan (TTP)'s foiled but potentially lethal attempts on Christmas Day 2009 over Detroit and May 2010 in Times Square.[8]

Many factors beyond weak intelligence capabilities contribute to the Boko Haram insurgency. Supporters believe that the West is a corrupting influence on Nigerian governance and society.[9] Longstanding political and economic competition between Christian Igbo tribes and Muslim Hausa and Yoruba elite over the country's oil wealth also fuels intense rivalry.[10] The failure by the government to successfully address socio-economic problems and unemployment in Nigeria leads many to violence.[11] Despite a $2,700 annual per capita income and 7% GDP growth, 70% of Nigerians live on less than $1.25/day.[12] In the north, 72% live in poverty compared to 27% in the south and 35% in the oil-rich and predominantly Christian Niger Delta region.[13] Lastly, the government's failure to prosecute security and police forces that engage in excessive force and executions of Boko Haram followers, leads to a continuous cycle of retaliatory attacks.[14] While these attacks currently affect Nigerian citizens, the U.S. has a vested interest in a stable Nigeria.

The United States' relationship with Nigeria is the most strategic relationship on the continent, and its stabilization is essential in meeting U.S. Theater Strategic Objectives.[15] In addition to being America's fifth largest supplier of oil, Nigeria also produces most of the hydrocarbon in West Africa which attracts American investment. The quality of crude oil from Nigeria is easily adapted to U.S. refineries, lessening U.S. dependence on the Middle Eastern supply.[16] Boko Haram could potentially disrupt U.S. access to this new source of oil and cause billions of dollars in damage to the U.S. economy. To put this threat into perspective, a much smaller militant group with minimal outside support, the Movement for the Emancipation of the Niger Delta (MEND), managed to significantly disrupt Nigeria's oil production by 25% in two years through intermittent attacks against the petroleum industry.[17]

Additionally, Nigeria is the lead peacekeeping nation in Africa and the founder of the Economic Community of West African States (ECOWAS). Nigeria was invaluable in bringing peace and stability to civil war-torn Liberia, Rwanda, and other nations. If the Boko Haram destabilizes Nigeria, the entire region could collapse. Restoring stability would require a robust and long-term commitment, similar to, or possibly more significant than the commitment made to Iraq and Afghanistan, in terms of troops, time, and money. Additionally, Nigeria is the transshipment point for approximately one-third of the heroin seized by authorities in the United States.[18] Such a rampant drug trade both finances potential terrorist acts against the U.S. and negatively affects many elements of U.S. society.

Lastly, the Boko Haram has the potential to harm U.S. citizens due to confirmed training and financial support from Al-Qaeda. At a meeting of security leaders from the ECOWAS nations, the Nigerian Chief of Staff of the armed forces confirmed for the first time that Al-Qaeda in the Islamic Maghreb (AQIM) provides support and training to Boko Haram.[19] General Ham, the AFRICOM commander stated, "What is most worrying at present is, at least in my view, a clearly stated intent by Boko Haram and by al-Qaeda in the Islamic Maghreb to coordinate and synchronize their efforts...I think it would be the most dangerous thing to happen not only to the Africans, but to us as well."[20]   Properly structured, ETs led

by AFRICOM could prevent such collaboration.

ENGAGEMENT TEAM FRAMEWORK

The Engagement Team (ET) concept is based on the Provincial Reconstruction Teams

(PRTs) utilized in Iraq and Afghanistan to interact with and influence the local

populace. According to FM 3-24, *Counterinsurgency*, "PRTs were conceived as a means to

extend the reach and enhance the legitimacy of the central government."[21]   ETs would

greatly assist in "winning the hearts and minds" of Nigerians in the north who harbor

negative sentiments against the predominantly southern run government.

It is critical that any outside footprint remain minimal due to the deep seated effects of

colonialism, a strong resistance to U. S. occupation, and Nigeria's leading role as the premier

country in West Africa. On 29 February 2012, Gen. Ham reaffirmed AFRICOM's

commitment to a small footprint while still countering terrorist threats.[22] In secure areas in

Afghanistan, PRTs were able to maintain a low profile.[23] ETs in Nigeria would do the same

both in composition and interaction with society. ETs in Nigeria should consist of 20-30

man teams dispersed throughout various states, but predominantly in the north. It is

imperative that the team contain at least a 50% Nigerian composition, including local state

citizens, police, military and both Islamic and Christian religious leaders. Including an

equitable mix of both U.S. and Nigerian forces on ETs accomplishes the AFRICOM

objective of strengthening defense capabilities of key African states and sustains direct

Nigerian involvement against Boko Haram. The remaining fifty percent of the team should

consist of U.S. military Chaplains, Intelligence, Ordnance, Corps of Engineers,

Administrative, Logistics, Civil Affairs, and Special Forces personnel, agents from the FBI and CIA, U.S. Agency for International Development (USAID), Department of Homeland Security (DHS), Department of Justice (DoJ) and USDA employees. The confluence of representatives from the aforementioned agencies would enable AFRICOM to bilaterally neutralize the foundations of Boko Haram. While optimal team composition enhances performance, command and control is a critical function of any operation.

Engagement Teams for Nigeria should have an AFRICOM operational commander at the helm. Currently, AFRICOM is the only one of these participating agencies with an interagency staff of its own. Hence, AFRICOM should provide the operational commander, regardless of whether this person is military or civilian. Additionally, AFRICOM, as a geographic combatant command, has the best access to relevant lessons learned from PRTs in Afghanistan and Iraq. However, the Ambassador to Nigeria, as the U.S. President's personal representative, would have ultimate decision-making authority (See Appendix B for proposed ET structure/rationale). Once approved by all participating agencies, ETs can begin preparations to increase intelligence collection from the populace, reduce sectarian rivalry, and promote self-sustainment in order to eradicate the root problems that perpetuate Boko Haram.

ETS: THE MISSING LINK TO ACTIONABLE INTEL

Engagement teams would provide a critical link between villagers and police and counterterrorism groups by creating avenues for Nigerian citizens to report observed terrorist activity. Often times the most pertinent information comes from the grass root level but never reaches appropriate authorities.[24] Only after attacks occur do Nigerian forces respond swiftly and forcefully against members of Boko Haram. Without a strong intelligence collection program, the funding, training, and leadership structures within Boko Haram will remain an enigma to Nigerian counterterrorism forces. Current barriers to gathering

information on Boko Haram include the fact that many national forces hail from the south

and share no ethnic or cultural ties with the northern population.[25] Also, those sympathetic to

the Boko Haram withhold knowledge of Boko Haram activity. President Jonathan lamented

that there are members of his government and security agencies that inhibit the gathering and

safekeeping of relevant intelligence.[26] The extent of such corruption runs deep. Following

the Christmas Day bombings of churches outside Abuja, Nigerian forces arrested the

mastermind, Kabir Sokoto, while he was taking refuge at the luxury lodge of the Borno State

governor. Sokoto escaped while under the guard of Zakari Biu, who was once ousted from

the police force for attacking political opponents; he is presently the Head of the Police anti-

terrorism unit.[27] These issues are reminiscent of obstacles the U.S. countered with success in

previous foreign conflicts.

The Civil Operations and Rural Development and Support (CORDS) program employed

by the U.S. during Vietnam offers valuable lessons in bridging the gap between interagency

teams and the local populace. CORDS intertwined civilian, military and the local populace

to accomplish non-military functions during the Vietnam War.[28] One lesson learned from

CORDS is the importance of directly attacking the enemy's center of gravity: its ability to

remain among the population.[29] In Vietnam, the Viet Cong used a mixture of promises of

reform and violent threats to usurp control over the local population.[30] The military and

civilian teams of CORDS under the direction of the CIA initiated a program entitled

Intelligence Coordination and Exploitation (ICEX), later named Phoenix. The teams built

district intelligence and operations coordinating centers (DIOCCs) to collect, disseminate,

and forward critical information to field units.[31] The Phoenix program, though sometimes abused, rooted out the Vietcong's stronghold by focusing on securing the population and developing self-defense and local self-governance capability.[32] The program increased intelligence gathering by bringing former Vietcong fighters into the fold of the interagency teams. The Marine Corp's Combined Action Program (CAP) increased grassroots intelligence by embedding a combined Marine/indigenous platoon among the locals. CAP prevented guerillas from convincing the population to provide sanctuary.[33]

The Boko Haram's ability to freely move throughout the north enables their capability to exercise the principle of surprise in their attacks. Similar to ICEX/Phoenix, specialized intelligence centers for collection and analysis of reports from the local populace would significantly prepare authorities to thwart planned attacks. By employing ETs that consist of U.S. intelligence experts and highly vetted Nigerian counterparts, the potential of operational leaks to Boko Haram members would diminish. By directly engaging the local populace and establishing ongoing relationships with tribal and community leaders, ETs would slowly earn the trust and allegiance of the people. To gradually begin forming this alliance, the ET would dress in the local garb and practice daily customs. Similar to President Bush's decision to appease African nations by making General Ward, an African-American, the first AFRICOM commander, Nigerian ETs would initially consist of Nigerian and other African-Americans, as much as possible. This is a necessary measure. During an interview with Captain Frederick Ogu, a U.S. Naval War College student from the Nigerian Navy, he stated that due to the negative effects of colonialism and both Islamic and African sentiments towards occupation by the U.S., race does matter to West Africans.[34]

The 1961 version of "Military Operations against Irregular Forces" recommends that troops remain in the same operational area for an extended period to reap maximum benefits.[35] ETs would garner success by hiring vetted local civilians to work with the ET due to their familiarity with the population, terrain, and language.[36] The U.S. component of the ETs would remain for an extended period of time to gather sufficient intelligence on Boko Haram members and sufficiently develop their Nigerian counterparts.

The aforementioned measures would drastically limit the Boko Haram's ability to continue discrete operations among the northern Nigerian population; however, actions must also be taken to counteract safe havens and tolerance outside of Nigeria. According to COIN expert Robert Cassidy, "Counterinsurgents cannot prevail if they allow the existence of insurgent sanctuaries."[37] Insurgents use border nations to smuggle persons, weapons, and equipment. ETs would help eliminate sanctuaries in bordering nations. The DHS would provide much needed training in border security, as indigenous forces are best suited to identify foreign actors.[38] In Tal afar, Iraq, both U.S. Soldiers and Iraqi security forces isolated insurgents from external support by controlling the border areas and constructing an eight-foot berm around the city.[39] The porous northern borders Nigerians share with Chad and Niger are sanctuaries for the Boko Haram and recruiting grounds for radical Muslims.[40] A focus area of Security Cooperation is Assurance and Regional Confidence Building. ETs should bolster intelligence capabilities of neighboring nations as well. While debate surrounds U.S. relations with Pakistan and India, cooperation from both nations undeniably enhanced U.S. efforts to counter insurgents from Afghanistan. A transnational program could flourish along Nigeria's borders as well; Niger and Chad would likely participate due to Nigeria's overarching influence in the region.

ETs: Instilling Nationalism Amid the Threat of Bifurcation

Engagement Teams would diminish the longstanding rivalry between moderate Muslims and Christians in Nigeria. A spirit of cooperation would develop from ET negotiations with local and national governments to address grievances of moderate Muslims and work towards a more equitable government representation. The north is not a monolithic Muslim society. ETs would unite the efforts of Christian and Muslim northerners by providing the opportunity to work side-by-side to enhance the paltry conditions of their region. Resulting improvements from this unity of effort would foster nationalism.

Six decades of colonial rule resulted in the creation of a disjointed Nigeria with over 250 ethnic groups and 500 indigenous languages. The British and French did not maintain territorial integrity along ethnic lines and separated groups that fell under the Sokoto Caliphate, with 80% falling under British control in Nigeria.[41] This division is important in that the Sultan of Sokoto, the nation's prominent de facto leader, is still the most influential leader for over 80 million Nigerian Muslims and millions in border countries.[42] This contributes to the problem of porous borders and foreigners both harboring the Boko Haram and joining the terrorist organization. The British also made Nigeria the model for indirect rule by governing through Fulani emirs in the north, hence northerners became accustomed to holding power.[43] Secondary to its aim of Islamic Rule in Nigeria, the Boko Haram threatened bifurcation by forming a separate Islamic state. Many northerners support a separate state due to minimal government representation which results from educational disparities, religious differences, and nepotism.[44] However, evidence of success in bridging the gap between divergent groups to increase nationalist sentiments exists right in West Africa.

In the war-torn nation of Liberia, religious leaders recognized that civil society organizations were crucial to peace.[45] The Liberian Council of Churches and the National Muslim Council of Liberia formed the Inter-Faith Mediation Committee (IFMC) for the sole purpose of war termination. In Africa, many social services come from spiritual institutions; warring factions benefited from these services during their lives. While initially unsuccessful at ending the conflict, the IFMC became the only credible neutral organization in Liberia and it was under its model that ECOWAS used the IFMC and other civil society groups under its auspices to end Liberia's first civil war.[46]

Utilizing ETs to diminish popular support for Boko Haram and to unify Christians and Muslims would work for two reasons: first, ETs could identify and exploit the divide between modern and radical Muslims and second, ETs would foster a mutual understanding through dialogue and actions that establish equality. Contrary to Boko Haram's tactics of spreading Islam by force, the Sultan of Sokoto recently condemned the Boko Haram and recommended a program of local monitoring that strengthened the power of the Hakimai (district heads) and employed youth leaders to detect strange people and activity in their local areas.[47]

Among Muslim Nigerians, there are traditional followers of the Sultan of Sokoto who espouse peace, yet there are those who align or at least sympathize with the Boko Haram. The Boko Haram publicly vowed to render violence against the Sultan of Sokoto and other senior Muslim leaders if they did not advocate for the release of some of their captured members.[48] Making threats against the prime Islamic leader hardened this divide. ETs and the government could exploit this divergence to unite moderate Muslims and Christians into a nation that desires peace and religious freedom. Together, Muslim and Christian leaders within the ET would hear and resolve grievances. Unity of effort is not only important for the RT, but also fosters tolerance amid the two groups and dissolves support for a solely Islamic state. The government's willingness to allow AFRICOM to employ a solution that incorporates all aspects of DIME, vice solely using force, would be seen by the people as progress.

Another step towards peaceful coexistence would be to understand the legitimate aspect of complaints that gave rise to Boko Haram. Poverty in northern Nigeria caused an increase in crime beyond the capacity of law enforcement.[49] Their call for the enforcement of Sharia law is, in Boko Haram's view, the best way to preserve, protect and direct their people. However, once the ETs began developing their areas, moderate Muslims would recognize that there is a peaceful way to gain protection and equality.

Though seemingly hopeless at times, African communities have the capacity to promote mutual understanding and coexist peacefully through the use of unofficial strategies such as prayer and communal solidarity.[50] Employing these traditional strategies with developed conflict management processes that the U.S. would bring in the form of an ET would be a major catalyst for peace. However, without a means to support one's self many Nigerians would still join or support the Boko Haram in exchange for basic necessities.

ETs: PROMOTING SELF-SUSTAINMENT

Engagement Teams would promote self-sustainment in impoverished areas of Nigeria in order to diminish the desire to participate and/or support terrorism as a way out of poverty. Boko Haram followers consist of hundreds of poor young northerners, students and professionals who are mostly unemployed.[51] By closing the disparity gap between the north and south, fewer people would align with Boko Haram. Across Africa, prostitution and child soldiering are ways to make money. Often, terrorist groups will provide food and shelter in exchange for carrying out such acts. ETs would provide attractive alternatives to this dastardly fate by teaching trade and technical skills, developing schools and providing even the most basic opportunities. United States agencies successfully increased opportunities for self-sustainment using PRTs in Afghanistan.

The USDA sponsored a program in which Afghan farmers flew to the U.S to develop modern and economically sufficient farming practices. ETs in Nigeria could work directly with the local populace to develop farming techniques. While the South has the bountiful resource of oil on its side, the North must rely on agricultural and industrial development. In Afghanistan, the contribution of the USDA resulted in the installation of windmills to pump water for irrigation and livestock, treatment against parasites, and the establishment of nurseries and orchards to promote continued growth. This self-sustainment alleviated the need for Afghans to participate in the drug trade and support terrorism.[52]

By allowing an ET to neutrally assist in securing lucrative development deals for Northern Nigeria, there would be an influx of much needed income and jobs to Northerners. Unfortunately for Liberia, there was no outside assistance when the government coordinated a deal with the Firestone Rubber Company in which the pay and conditions did little to positively develop the nation at large. Islamic banks are also a new source of revenue for Northern Nigeria.[53] With the assistance of the FBI and CIA, the Nigerian ET can ensure new Islamic banks are not financing terrorism and that a percentage of the revenue actual reaches the people. Both Renaissance Capital and Citigroup project Nigeria to be "one of the key generators of global growth over the next 40 years, with the potential to generate the highest real economic growth rate of 8.5% over the period."[54] The Boko Haram could easily stop Nigeria from reaching this great potential if allowed to persist.

COUNTERARGUMENT

While the arguments presented would yield significant benefits, the counterargument could be made that Nigeria's leadership would not be receptive to U.S. involvement in handling a Nigerian based terror organization. As the leading West African nation, Nigeria is proud of its sovereignty and accustomed to leading any assistance provided to its less capable neighbors. This sentiment was felt strongly when Nigeria and Algeria led opposition to AFRICOM placing its headquarters anywhere on African soil.[55] The African Union mantra "African Solutions to African Problems" is a deep rooted sentiment spawned by the negative effects of colonialism. This sentiment is so prevalent among Nigerians that Captain Ogu stood up and thanked CENTCOM's General Mattis for allowing Nigeria to handle the Boko Haram on its own during a briefing at the U.S. Naval War College. Additionally, U.S. involvement may have the blow-back result of increasing Boko Haram's alignment with al-Qaeda elements and make targeting U.S. interests a priority.

Another argument against the implementation of bilateral ETs is that the U.S. would not want to fund an expensive operation for a terror organization with seemingly local aims while recovering from the financial and emotional toll of two simultaneous wars. With pressing domestic priorities, including protecting U.S. borders and unemployment, U.S. citizens and government officials might prefer a robust UN solution vice direct U.S. intervention. In addition, any U.S. military casualties as a result of U.S. engagement with Boko Haram would be largely unpopular at home.

REBUTTAL

While the counterarguments present logical concerns, actions already taken by the U.S. and Nigeria invalidate these considerations and demonstrate the feasibility of implementing ETs. After the UN bombing, the Nigerian government specifically requested U.S. assistance to defeat Boko Haram. This shows that the Nigerian government realizes the limits of their current capabilities. Nigerian officials are smartly seizing upon the United States' experience in fighting terror over the last eleven years. ETs would collectively capture and implement derived best practices. With a small footprint, AFRICOM ETs would not garner the negative reactions associated with "boots on the ground."

Lastly, the United States is clearly willing to fund operations that will secure their most strategic partner in Africa and ultimately protect U.S. citizens. Access to an oil supply outside of the Middle East is crucial to the U.S. economy. Hence, Nigeria is already among the top ten recipients of U.S. foreign aid dollars. A successful outcome would ultimately allow a greater partnership with Nigeria resulting in a positive return on funds invested to combat Boko Haram. Also, with Nigeria leading peacekeeping operations throughout the continent, it behooves the U.S. to keep Nigeria viable to continue the status quo.

RECOMMENDATIONS

ETs are a clear and effective solution to achieve sustained stability in Nigeria. The first step is for current U.S. leaders in Nigeria to gain concurrence from both national and local government leaders in the north by thoroughly and diplomatically explaining the components and actions of an ET. Secondly, ETs must arrive as a cohesive group. The team must train together prior to their deployment to Northern Nigeria. The training should be mandatory and standardized so that each ET has a baseline for the conduct of operations throughout the region. As much as possible, AFRICOM should send Nigerian ET members to the U.S. to train with the team, especially religious leaders. This would also ensure the entire ET truly understands the plight of the people. Furthermore, AFRICOM should establish meetings for the ET with former PRT members for first-hand experience as seemingly small mistakes could derail mission accomplishment. PRTs in Afghanistan often lacked the requisite number of interagency personnel. All participating government agencies should choose personnel with the maturity, professional expertise, and cultural understanding to operate in Nigeria and provide attractive incentives to increase the pool of volunteers. And finally, it is important that AFRICOM synchronize the deployments to keep an ET together as long as possible for optimal results.[56]

CONCLUSION

The United States and other nations utilize PRTs for post-conflict stabilization; however, Engagement Teams in Nigeria would pre-empt an all-out war that could potentially destabilize the entire region and block access to key U.S. interests. Efforts by the Nigerian government to end the horrors brought about by the Islamic radicals of Boko Haram are simply not broad enough in scope to truly eradicate the roots of this insurgency. A purely military solution will not work. Rife with religious, economic and ethnic strife, corruption and many other traits of a failed state, Nigeria is still an emerging power. With the skill set of a bilateral Engagement Team, Nigeria can eradicate the Boko Haram and realize its full potential as a leading nation, not only in West Africa, but across the entire continent and beyond.

Figure 1. **MAP OF NIGERIA BY STATE**

Figure 2. **ENGAGEMENT TEAM COMPOSITION**

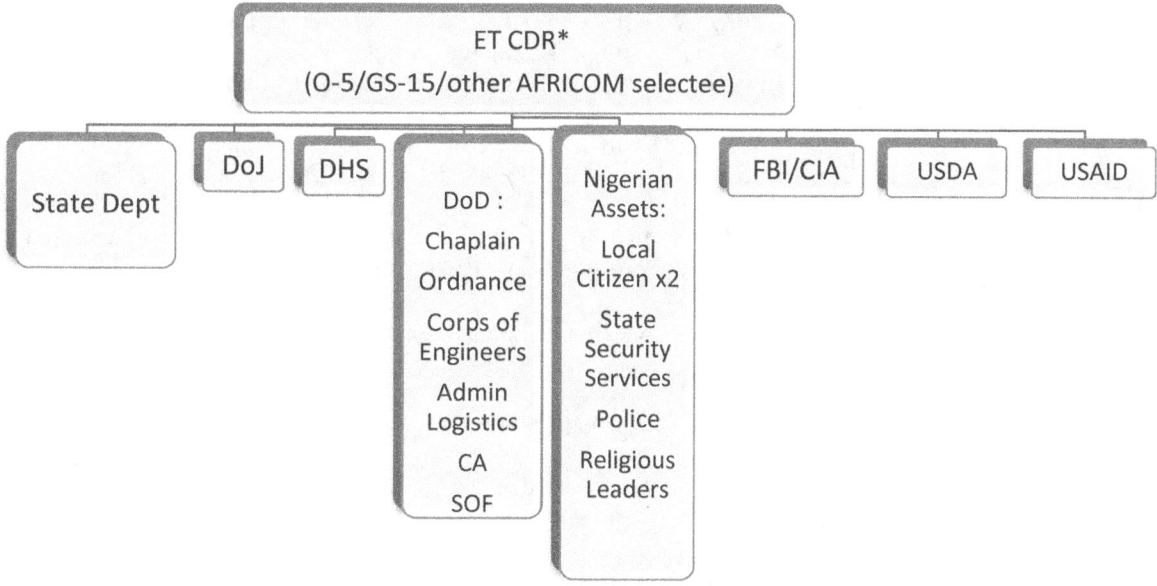

*The ET Commander would be responsible for gaining approval for all actions through the Ambassador/Chief of Mission to Nigeria <u>and</u> the AFRICOM chain of command. The AFRICOM leadership would address any issues with the Ambassador should differences arise. The Ambassador makes the final decision as the POTUS representative.

The State Department Rep. would be responsible for negotiations with the local and national government and ensuring all actions align with the approved Mission Plan for Nigeria.

The Department of Justice Rep. would develop a Nigerian model for the fair prosecution of terrorists and assist in teaching Nigerian law enforcement about proportionality.

The Department of Homeland Security would train Nigerians Assets on the fundamentals of border security due to the porous borders in the North and neighboring fragile nations.

DoD assets would fulfill traditional roles per Military Occupational Specialty.

Nigerian assets would consist of local citizens, State Security Services and Police. All of whom would have to be highly vetted and monitored to avoid corruption. Religious leaders would include both Christian and Muslim leaders with knowledge of tribal religions as well.

The FBI/CIA would direct, train and establish sound intelligence procedures.

The USDA would assist in developing the cotton, cocoa, palm oil and rubber industries in the north.

USAID would develop the school and healthcare infrastructure and programs.

NOTES

[1] U.S. President George W. Bush, *The National Security Strategy of the United States of America,* (Washington, DC: White House, 2002): 41, quoted in Peter J. Pham, "Next Front? Evolving United States-African Strategic Relations in the "War on Terrorism" and Beyond," doi: 10.1080/01495930701271536.

[2] Peter J. Pham, "Next Front? Evolving United States-African Strategic Relations in the 'War on Terrorism' and Beyond." *Comparative Strategy*, 26 (2007): 46, doi:10.1080/01495930701271536.

[3] U.S. Africa Command, *U.S. Africa Command Fact Sheet,* September 2, 2010, accessed 01 April 2012, http://www.africom.mil/fetchBinary.asp?pdfID=20101109171627.

[4] Scott Stewart, "Nigeria's Boko Haram Militants Remain a Regional Threat," *Stratfor Weekly,* accessed 13 April 2012, http://www.stratfor.com/weekly/nigerias-boko-haram-militantsremain-a-regional-threat.

[5] Guide 2 Nigeria, accessed 20 April 2012, http:// www.guide2nigeria.com/information/14/Borno-State.

[6] Babjee Pothuraju, "Boko Haram's Persistent Threat in Nigeria," *The Backgrounder*, http://www.idsa.in/system/files/ThreatInNigeria_BabjePothuraju.pdf.

[7] *Jane's Islamic Affairs Analyst,* "Boko Haram moves closer to AQIM," 22 March 2012, accessed 15 April 2012. Jane's Online.

[8] U.S. House Wants Boko Haram Designated Terrorist Group, (01 December 2009), accessed 13 April 2012, LexisNexis.

[9] Capt Frederick Ogu, Nigerian Navy, interview by the author in Newport, RI, 14 April 2012.

[10] Ibid.

[11] Ibid.

[12] Toni Johnson, "Boko Haram," *Backgrounder,* Council on Foreign Relations, last modified 27 December 2011, http://www.cfr.org/africa/boko-haram/p25739.

[13] Ibid.

[14] Ogu, Personal Interview.

[15] U.S. Department of State, *FY 2013 Mission Strategic and Resource Plan,* U.S. Mission to Nigeria(S/U), (Washington, DC: Department of State), 16 May 2011, 1.

[16] Pham, "Next Front," 44.

[17] *Jane's Intelligence Review,* "Delta force- Nigerian militant group's aims remain blurred," 16 April 2009, accessed 15 April 2012, Jane's Online.

[18] Pham, "Next Front," 47.

[19] *Jane's Intelligence Weekly,* "Nigerian security chief confirms Boko Haram links with Al-Qaeda," 24 February 2012, accessed 14 April 2012, Jane's Online.

[20] Jon Gambrell, "AP Interview: US General Sees Nigeria Terror Link," *ABC News,* 17 August 2012, http://ww.abcnews.go.com/International/t/story?id=143224228.

[21] U.S. Army and U.S. Marine Corps, *Counterinsurgency*, Field Manual (FM) 3-24/Marine Corps Warfighting Publication (MCWP) 3-33.5, (Washington, D.C.: Headquarters Department of the Army, December 2006), 2-12.

[22] Jan Childs, "AFRICOM's Gen Ham discusses Africa security before House committee," last modified 5 March 2012, http:// www.usaraf.army.mil/NEWS/NEWS_120305_HAM.html.

[23] U.S. Army and U.S. Marine Corps, *Counterinsurgency*, Field Manual (FM) 3-24/Marine Corps Warfighting Publication (MCWP) 3-33.5, (Washington, D.C.: Headquarters Department of the Army, December 2006), 2-12.

[24] Susanta Kumar Panda, et. al. "Counter Terrorism through Citizen's Intelligence Gathering & Intelligence Information Interlinking (CIGIII)," (National Informatics Centre: Orissa State, India), http://www.skoch.in/images/stories/security_paper_knowledge/Counter%20Terror.

[25] Pothuraju, "Persistent Threat," 7.

[26] Ibid.

[27] "Nigeria; Boko-Haram-Nation's Nightmare," The Nation (Nairobi), 9 February 2012, accessed 12 April 2012, LexisNexis, 4.

[28] *Jane's Online,* "Developing Disorder – Divergent PRT models in Afghanistan," 19 September 2008, accessed 13 April 2012, Jane's Online.

[29] Dale Andrade, "Three lessons from Vietnam," Washington Post, 28 December 2005, http:// www.washingtonpost.com/wp-dyn/content/article/2005/12/28/AR2005122801144.html.

[30] Ibid.

[31] Tucker, Spencer, "The Encyclopedia of the Vietnam War: A Political Social, and Military History," 909.

[32] Robert M. Cassidy, *Counterinsurgency and the Global War on Terror,* (Stanford: Stanford University Press, 2008), 137.

[33] Ibid., 138.

[34] Ogu, Personal Interview.

[35] Robert M. Cassidy, "US COIN Doctrine," *Small Wars Journal, (2008),* accessed 15 April 2012, *http://www.smallwarsjournal.com/mag/docs-temp/44-cassidy.pdf, 3.*

[36] Ibid., 3.

[37] Ibid., 1.

[38] Ibid., 3.

[39] U.S. Army and U.S. Marine Corps, FM 3-24/MCWP 3-33.5, 5-23.

[40] Ogu, Personal Interview.

[41] Anthony Asiwaju. *Transfrontier Regionalism: The European Union Perspective on Postcolonial Africa,* with *special Reference to Borgu*, (Vancouver: University of British Columbia Press, 1999), chap. 6, 128, http://books.google.com.

[42] Jonathan Beasley. "Sultan of Sokoto, Religious Leader of Nigeria's Muslim Community, to Visit Harvard," last modified 15 September 2011, under "search Sultan of Sokoto," http:// www.hds.harvard.edu.

[43] Martin Meredith, *The Fate of Africa.* (New York: Public Affairs, 2005), 6.

[44] Ogu, Personal Interview.

[45] Mike Oqaye. "The Liberian Crisis: Lessons for Intra-State Conflict Management and Prevention in Africa" (Institute for Conflict Analysis and Resolution, George Mason University, June 2001), 33, accessed 20 April 2012, http://scar.gmu.edu/wp_19_oquaye.pdf.

[46] Ibid., 34.

[47] Sahara Reporters, "We Must End Boko Haram, Says Sultan of Sokoto," 6 February 2012, http:// saharareporters.com/news-page/we-must-end-boko-haram-says-sultan-sokoto.

[48] Ndahi Marama, "We'll attack Sokoto, Boko Haram warns Sultan, Tambuwal, others," accessed 12 April 2012, http://www.vanguardngr.com/2012/well-attack-sokoto-boko-haram-warns-sultan-tambulwal-others/.

[49] Meredith, *The Fate of Africa,* 85.

[50] Akeem A. Akinwale, "Integrating the traditional and the modern conflict management strategies (paper presented as Faculty of Social Science, at the University of Ibadan, Nigeria, n.d.), 1.

[51] Nigeria Exchange, "Boko Haram," accessed 14 April 2012, http://www.ngex.com/nigeria/bokoharam.htm.

[52] United States Department of Agriculture, "Rebuilding Agriculture and Food Security in Afghanistan," accessed 12 April 2012, http:// www.fas.usda.gov/icd/drd/afghanistan.asp.

[53] Ogu, Personal Interview.

[54] Infrastructure Concession Regulatory Commission, "Addressing Infrastructure Deficit in Northern Nigeria," last modified March 2011, http://www.icrc.gov.ng/wp-content/uploads/2011/03/Northern_Economic_Summit_ICRC_March11.pdf, 46.

[55] Valerie Reed, "A Big Image Problem Down There: Prospects for an African Headquarters for AFRICOM," accessed 13 April 2012), http:// www.cdi.org/pdfs/reedafricom.pdf, 4.

[56] Nima Abbaszadeh, et. Al, "Provincial Reconstruction Teams: Lessons and Recommendations" (PowerPoint presentation, Princeton University, Woodrow Wilson School of Public & International Affairs, Princeton, NJ, January 2008), 18.

BIBLIOGRAPHY

Abbaszadeh, Nima, Mark Crow, Marianne El-Khoury, Jonathan Gandomi, David Kuwayama, Christopher MacPherson, Meghan Nutting, Nealin Parker, and Taya Weiss. "Provincial Reconstruction Teams: Lessons and Recommendations." PowerPoint presentation, Princeton University, Woodrow Wilson School of Public & International Affairs, Princeton, NJ, January 2008.

Akinwale, Akeem. "Integrating the traditional and the modern conflict management strategies in Nigeria." Paper presented as Faculty of the Department of Social Sciences, University of Ibadan, Nigeria. n.d.

Andrade, Dale. "Three lessons from Vietnam." *Washington Post.* 28 December 2005. http:// www.washingtonpost.com/wp- dyn/content/article/2005/12/28/AR2005122801144.html.

Asiwaju, Anthony. *Transfrontier Regionalism: The European Union Perspective on Postcolonial Africa, with special reference to Borgu.* Vancouver: University of British Columbia Press, 1999. http://books.google.com.

Beasley, Jonathan. "Sultan of Sokoto, Religious Leader of Nigeria's Muslim Community, to Visit Harvard." Last modified 15 September 2011. Under "Search Sultan of Sokoto," http://www.hds.harvard.edu.

Bush, George W. *The National Security Strategy of the United States of America.* Washington, DC: White House, 2002. Quoted in Peter J. Pham, "Next Front? Evolving United States-African Strategic Relations in the 'War on Terrorism' and Beyond." doi: 10.1080/01495930701271536.

Cassidy, Robert M. *Counterinsurgency and the Global War on Terror.* Stanford: Stanford University Press, 2008.

--- "US COIN Doctrine." *Small Wars Journal, (2008). http://www.smallwarsjournal.com/mag/docs-temp/44-cassidy.pdf 3.*

Childs, Jan. "AFRICOM's Gen Ham discusses Africa security before House committee." Last modified 5 March 2012. http:// www.usaraf.army.mil/NEWS/NEWS_120305_HAM.html.

Gambrell, Jon. "AP Interview: US General Sees Nigeria Terror Link." *ABC News,* 17 August 2011. http://ww.abcnews.go.com/International/t/story?id=143224228.

Guide2Nigeria. Accessed 20 Apr 2012. http://www.guide2nigeria.com/information/14/Borno-State.

Infrastructure Concession Regulatory Commission. "Addressing Infrastructure Deficit in Northern Nigeria." Last modified March 2011. http://www.icrc.gov.ng/nt/uploads/2011/03/Northern_Economic_Summit_ICRC_March11.pdf.

Jane's Intelligence Review. "Delta force- Nigerian militant group's aims remain blurred." 16 April 2009. Accessed 15 April 2012. Jane's Online.

Jane's Islamic Affairs Analyst. "Boko Haram moves closer to AQIM." 22 March 2012. Accessed 15 April 2012. Jane's Online.

Jane's Intelligence Weekly. "Nigerian security chief confirms Boko Haram links with Al-Qaeda." 24 February 2012. Accessed 14 April 2012. Jane's Online.

Jane's Online. "Developing Disorder – Divergent PRT models in Afghanistan." 19 September 2008. Accessed 13 April 2012. Jane's Online.

Johnson, Toni. "Boko Haram." *Backgrounder,* Council on Foreign Relations. Last modified 27 December 2011. http://www.cfr.org/africa/boko-haram/p25739.

Marama, Ndahi. "We'll attack Sokoto, Boko Haram warns Sultan, Tambuwal, others. " Vanguard. Accessed 12 April 2012. http://www.vanguardngr.com/2012/well-attack-sokoto-boko-haram-warns-sultan-tambulwal-others/.

Meredith, Martin. *The Fate of Africa.* New York: Public Affairs, 2005.

"Nigeria; Boko-Haram-Nation's Nightmare." *The Nation (Nairobi)*, 9 February 2012. Accesssed 10 April 2012. LexisNexis.

Oqaye, Mike. "The Liberian Crisis: Lessons for Intra-State Conflict Management and Prevention in Africa." Instititute for Conflict Analysis and Resolution. George Mason University, June 2001. http://scar.gmu.edu/wp_19_oquaye.pdf.

Pham, J. Peter. "Next Front? Evolving United States-African Strategic Relations in the 'War on Terrorism' and Beyond." *Comparative Strategy*, 26 (2007): 39-54. doi:10.1080/01495930701271536.

Panda, Susanta K., Hota, Ashok, Mohanty, Nilandri, and Mahapatra, Ashis. et. al. "Counter Terrorism through Citizen's Intelligence Gathering & Intelligence Information Interlinking (CIGIII)." National Informatics Centre: Orissa State, India. http://www.skoch.in/images/stories/security_paper_knowledge/Counter%20Terror.

Pothuraju, Babjee. "Boko Haram's Persistent Threat in Nigeria." *TheBackgrounder.* Accessed 09 April 2012. http://www.idsa.in/system/files/ThreatInNigeria_BabjePothuraju.pdf.

23

Reed, Valerie. "A Big Image Problem Down There: Prospects for an African Headquarters for AFRICOM." Accessed 13 April 2012. http:// www.cdi.org/pdfs/reedafricom.pdf.

Sahara Reporters, " We Must End Boko Haram, Says Sultan of Sokoto," 6 February 2012, http:// saharareporters.com/news-page/we-must-end-boko-haram-says-sultan-sokoto.

Stewart, Scott. "Nigeria's Boko Haram Militants Remain a Regional Threat." *Stratfor Weekly.* Accessed 13 April 2012. http://www.stratfor.com/weekly/nigerias-boko-haram- militants-remain-a-regional-threat.

U.S. Africa Command. *U.S. Africa Command Fact Sheet.* 2 September 2010. Accessed 01 April 2012. http://www.africom.mil/fetchBinary.asp?pdfID=20101109171627.

U.S. Army and U.S. Marine Corps, *Counterinsurgency*, Field Manual (FM) 3-24/Marine Corps Warfighting Publication (MCWP) 3-33.5. Washington, D.C.: Headquarters Department of the Army, December 2006.

U.S. Congress. House. Boko Haram Emerging Threat to the U.S. Homeland. Committee on Homeland Security, Subcommittee on Counterterrorism and Intelligence. Accessed 14 April 2012. http://homeland.house.gov/hearing/subcommittee-hearing-boko-haram-emerging-threat-us-homeland.

United States Department of Agriculture. "Rebuilding Agriculture and Food Security in Afghanistan." Accessed 12 April 2012. http://www.fas.usda.gov/icd/drd/afghanistan.asp.

U.S. Department of State, *FY 2013 Mission Strategic and Resource Plan,* U.S. Mission to Nigeria(S/U). Washington, DC: Department of State, 2011.

"U.S. House Wants Boko Haram Designated Terrorist Group." 01 December 2009. Accessed 13 April 2012. LexisNexis.